THIS COLORING WORKBOOK BELONGS TO

_____

Copyright Annie Anson
All right reserved

No part of this book may be reproduced by any mechanical. photographic or electronic process. The author of this book does not dispense medical advice or prescribe the use of any technique as a form of treatment for physical, emotional, or other medical problems

Paper Choice

We use standard-quality paper to balance affordability, accessibility, and durability. Standard-quality paper allows us to offer the book at a reasonable price, making it easy for everyone to enjoy. This type of paper is also designed to handle a variety of coloring materials, from colored pencils to crayons, and even some water-based markers.

By placing a Protective Sheet: For added peace of mind, place a blank sheet of paper behind the page you're working on. This will protect the following pages from any potential bleed-through.

Color Your World with Joy

Filling your world with joy through vibrant colors. Dive into a relaxing, creative escape where every page lets you express positivity and brighten your mood. Unleash your inner artist and watch happiness come to life, one color at a time!

Connect With Us

facebook page: Annieanson Coloring
facebook group: Annieansoncoloring

IG: annieanson_coloring

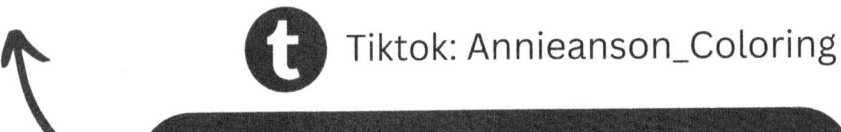

Tiktok: Annieanson_Coloring

JOIN US & GET FREE COLORING PAGES

Scan Me!
find more of our awesome collection!
Gave us some feedback

Visit our Instagram
@annieanson__coloring

coloring together!

Texture Sheet

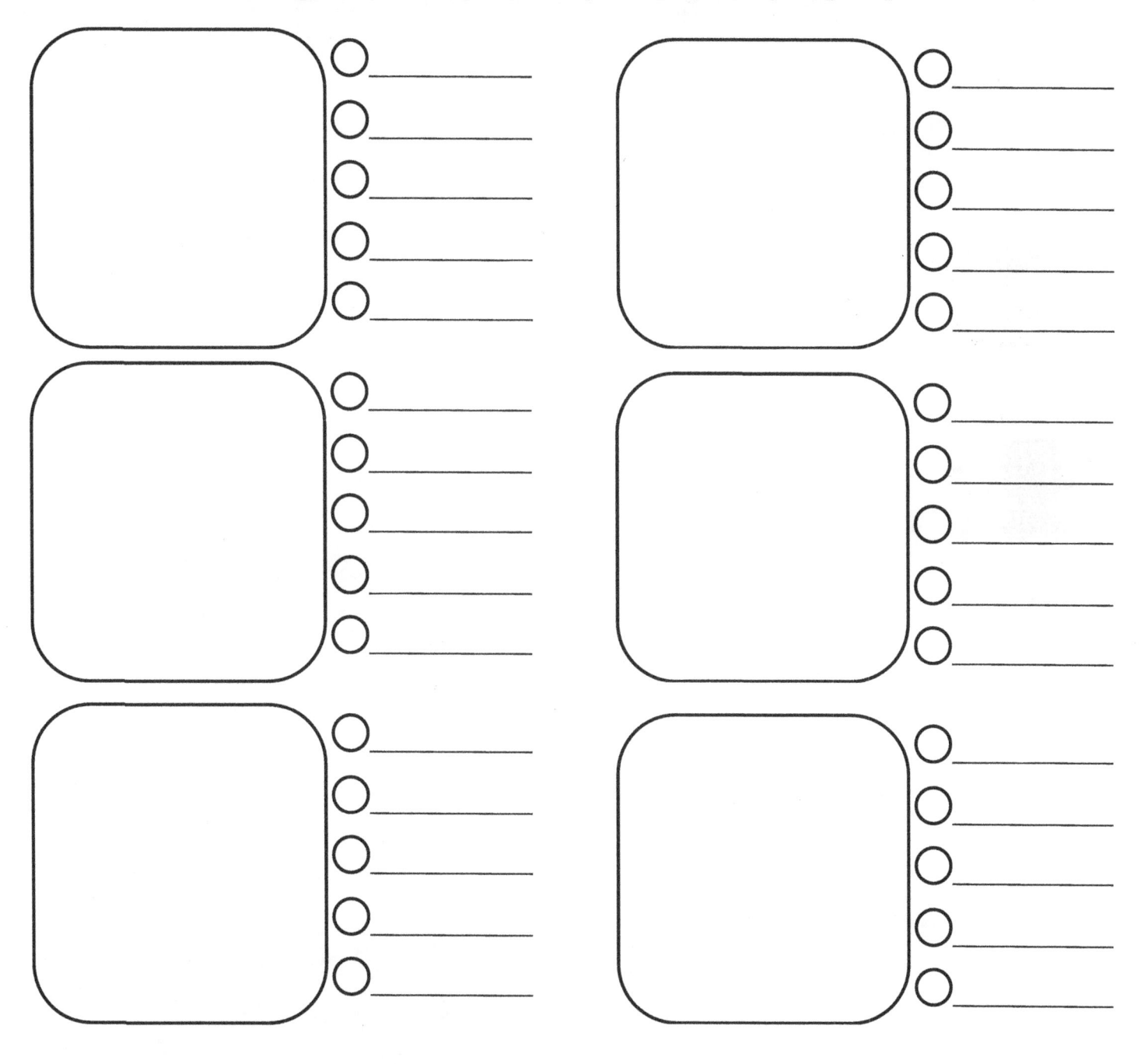

Texture Sheet

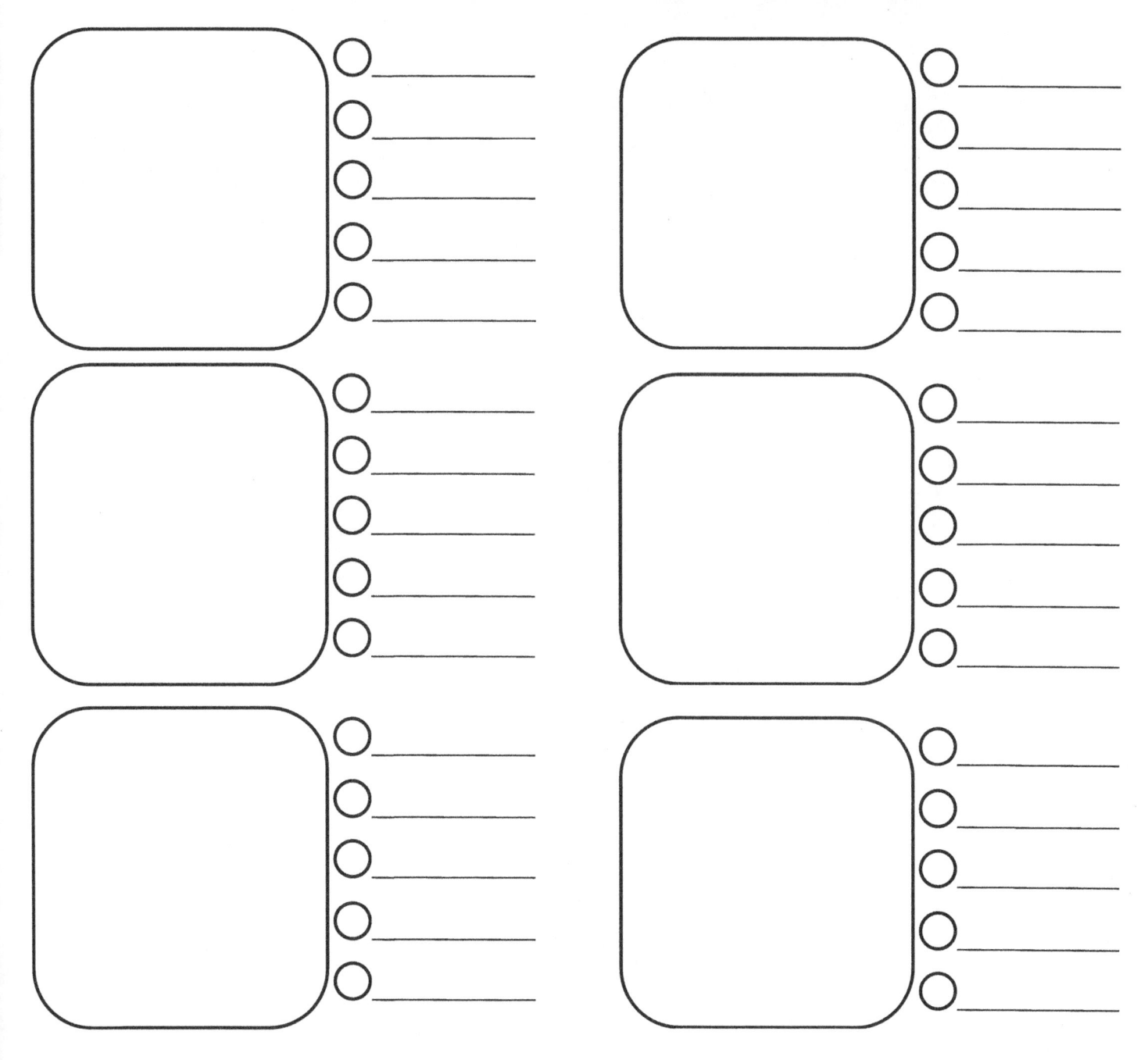

texture sheet

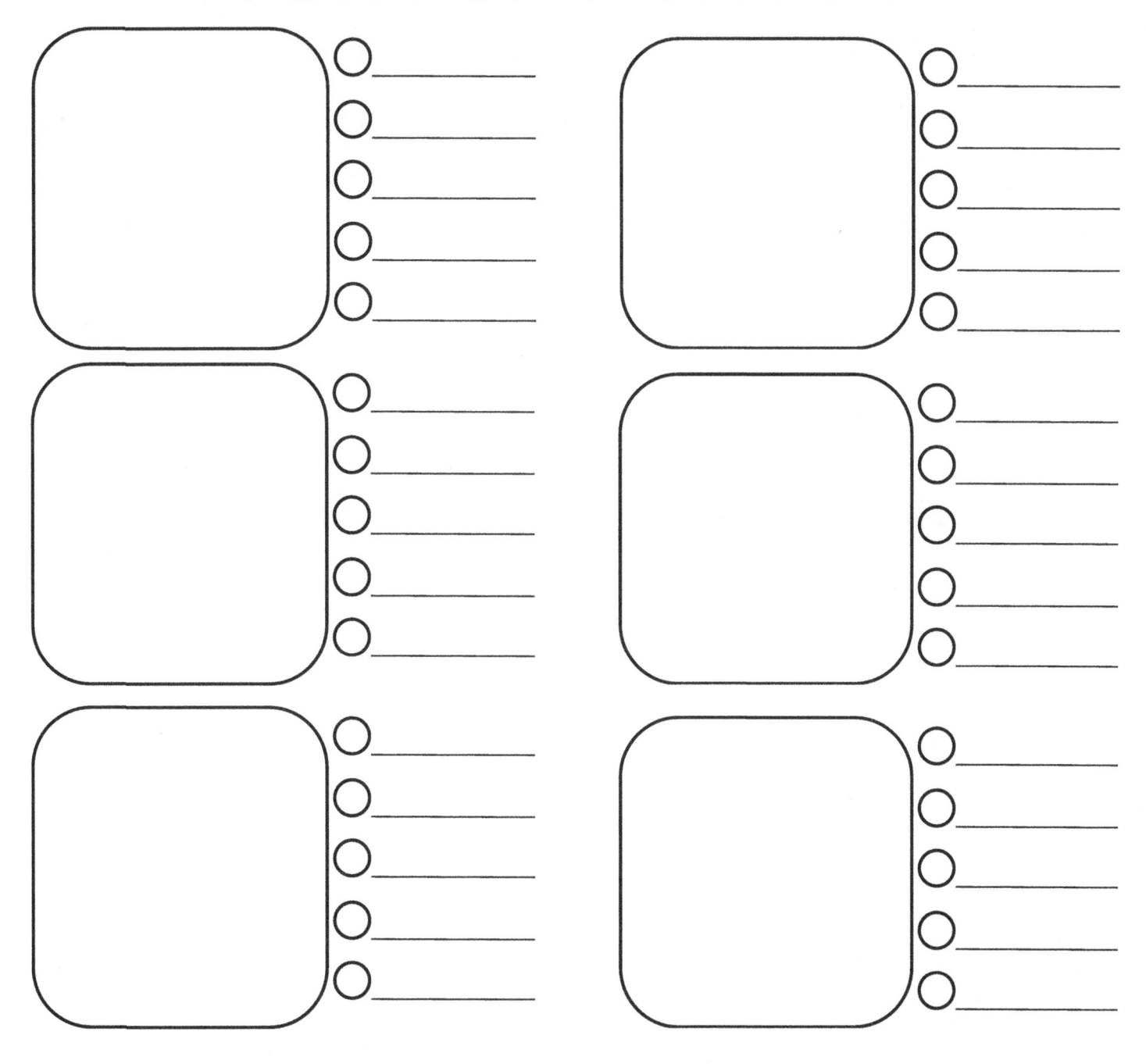

Texture Sheet

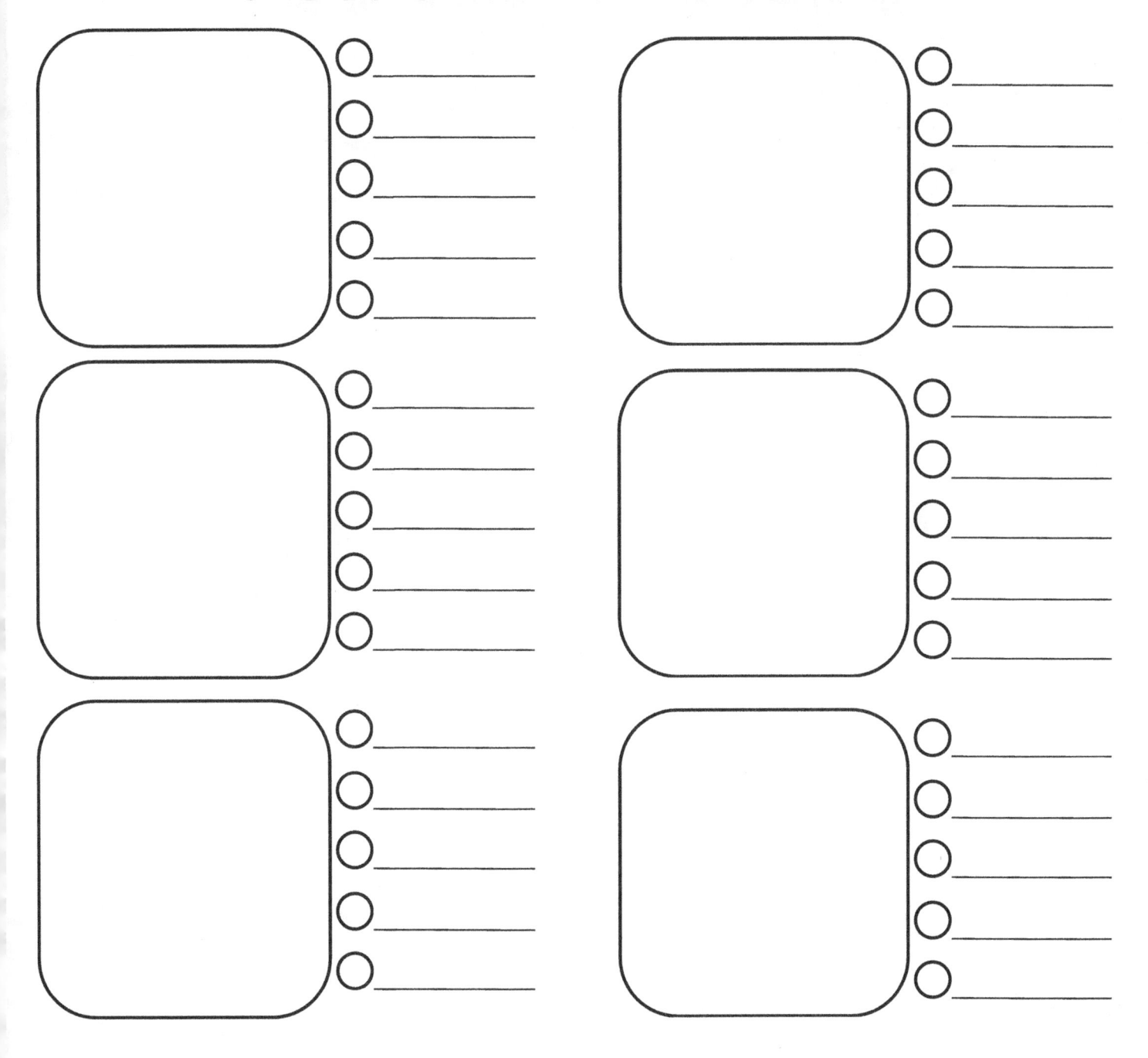

Gradient Sheet

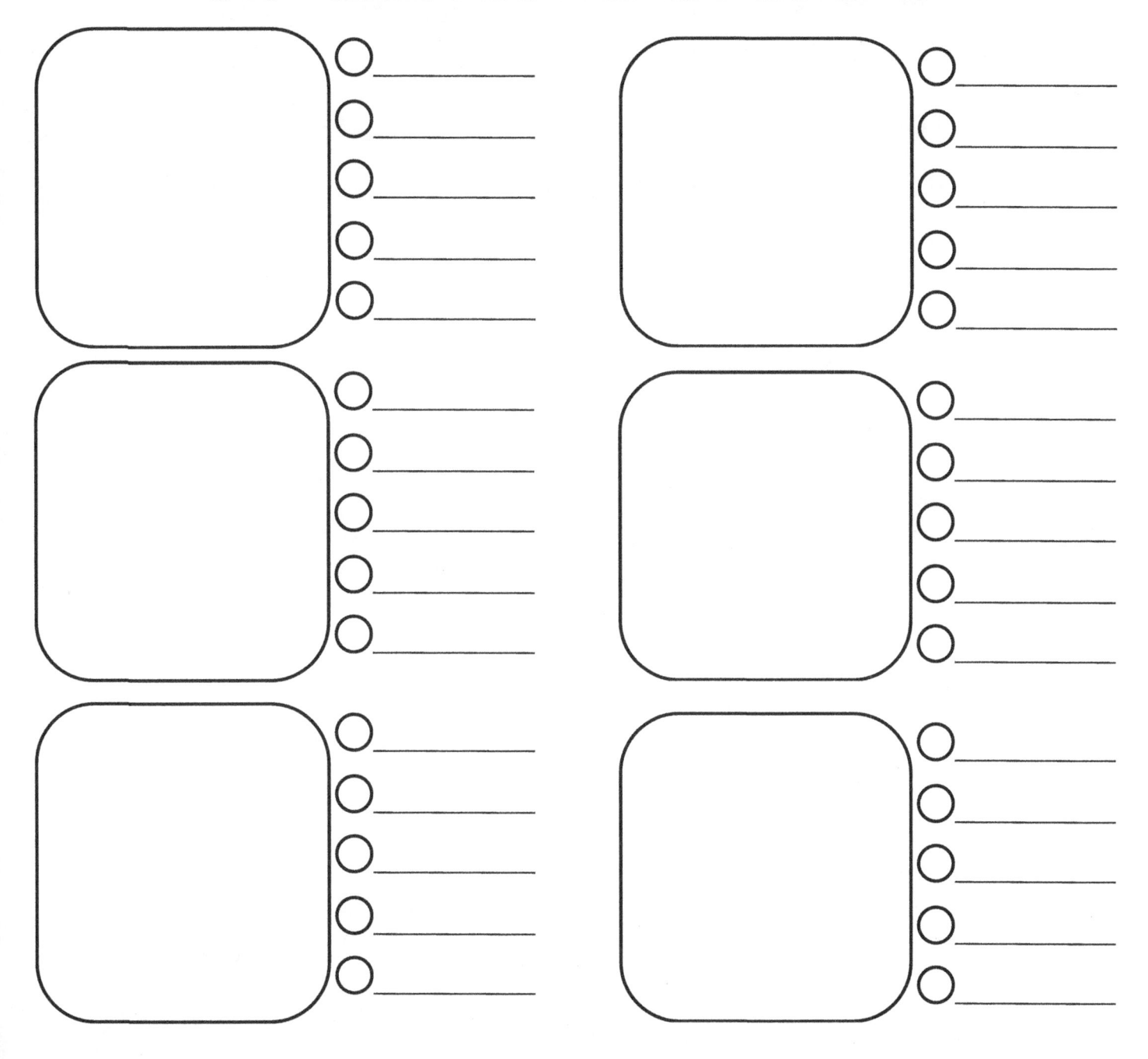

Gradient Sheet

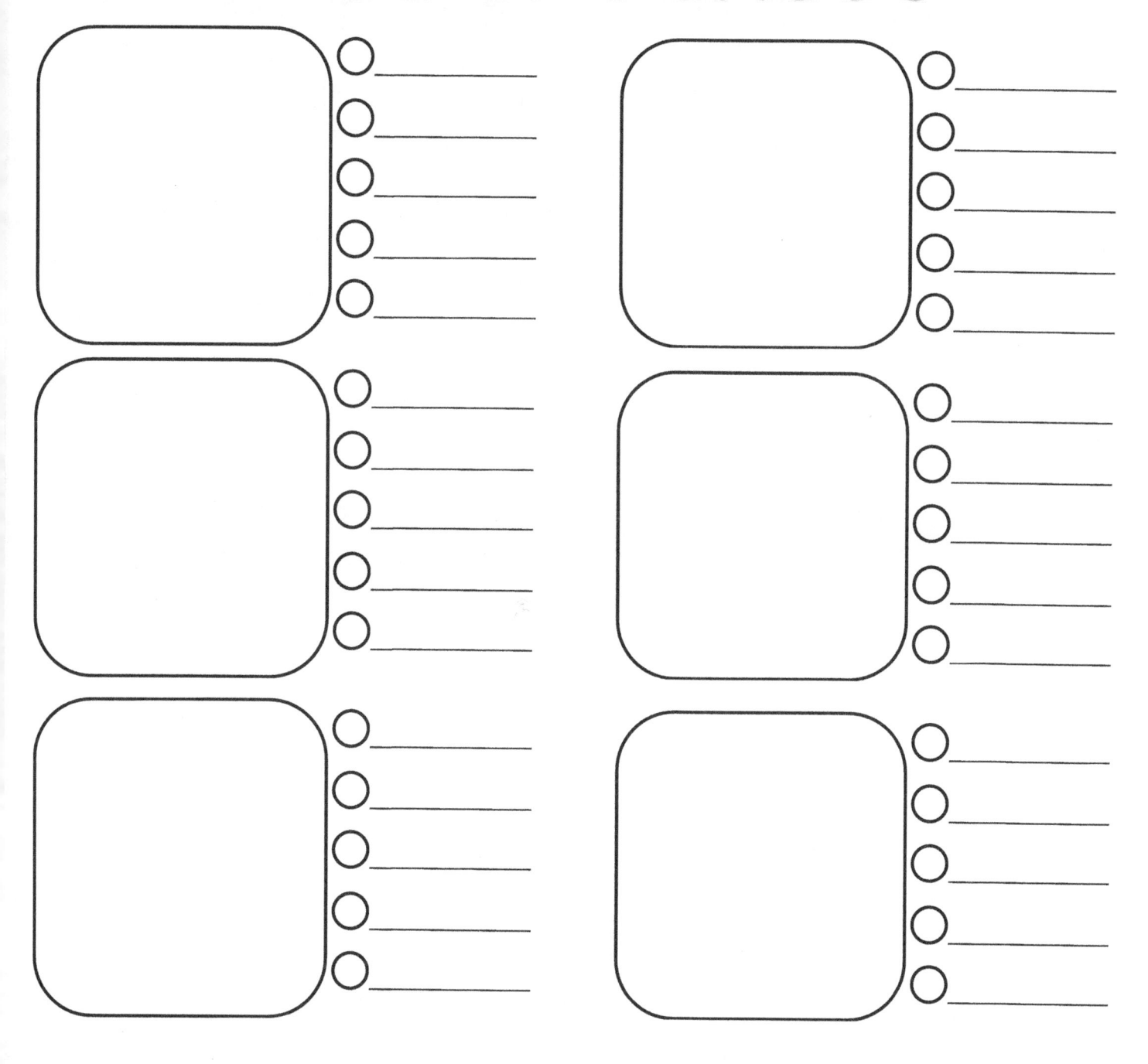

Gradient Sheet

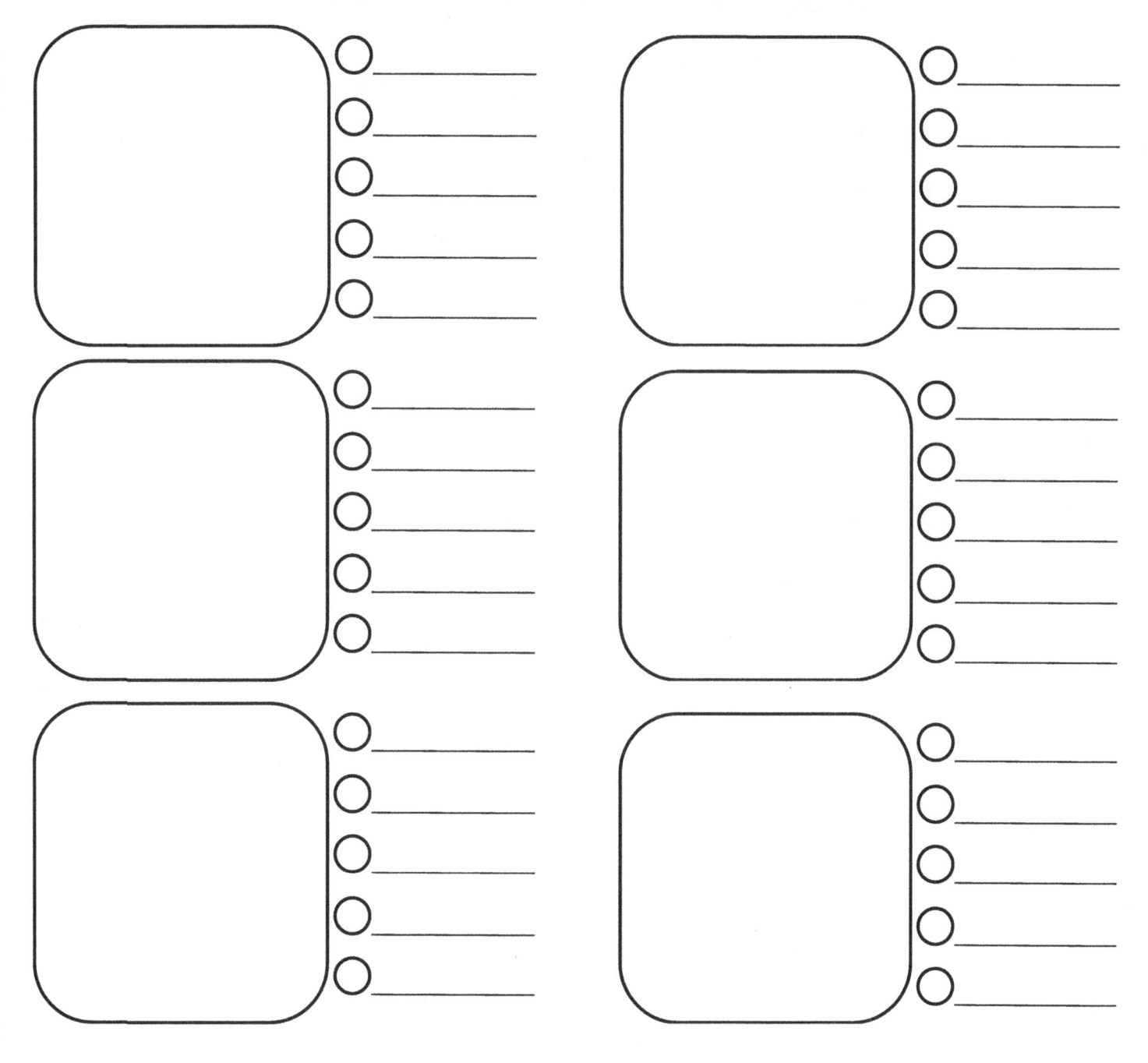

Gradient Sheet

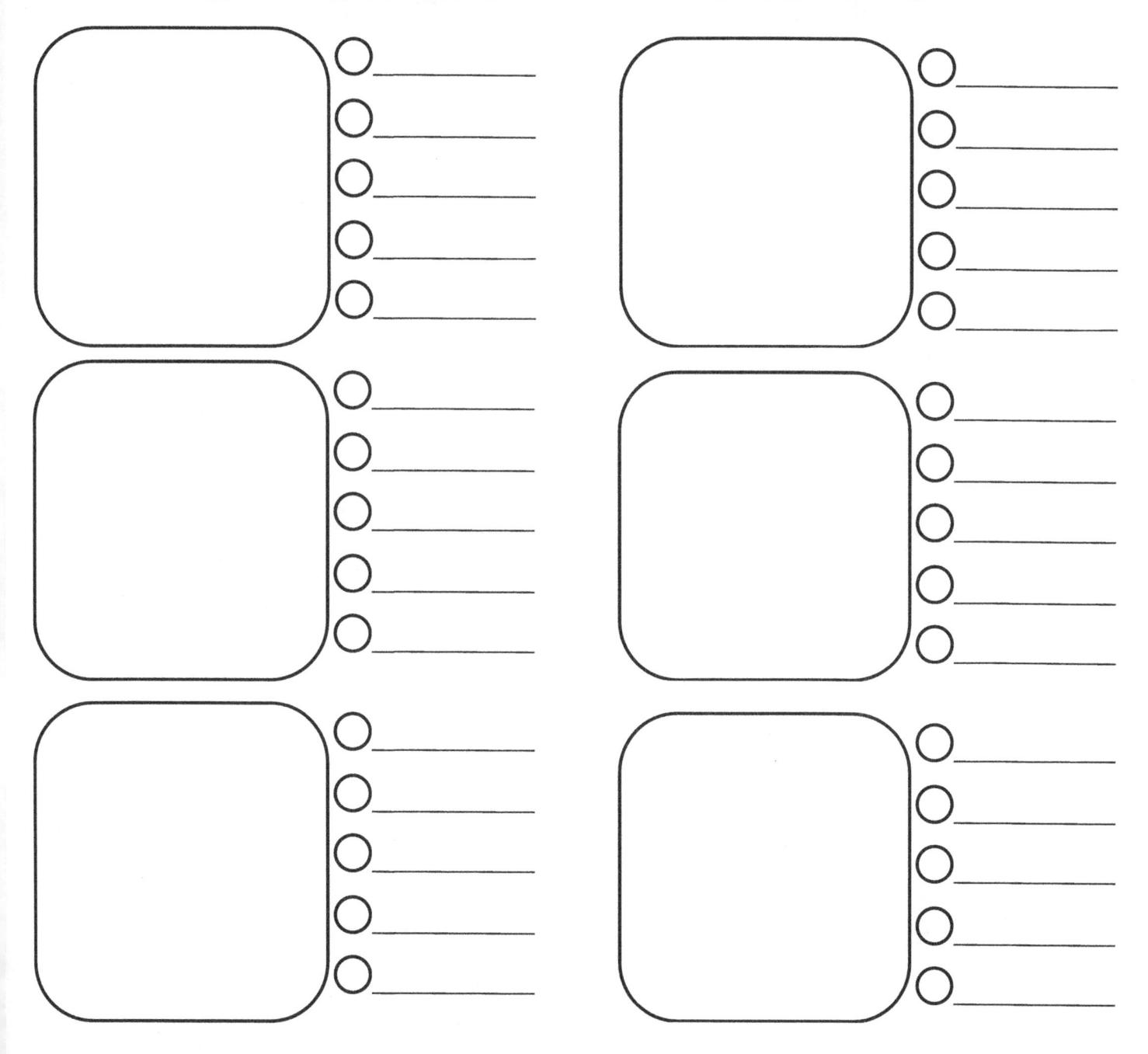

Pattern Sheet

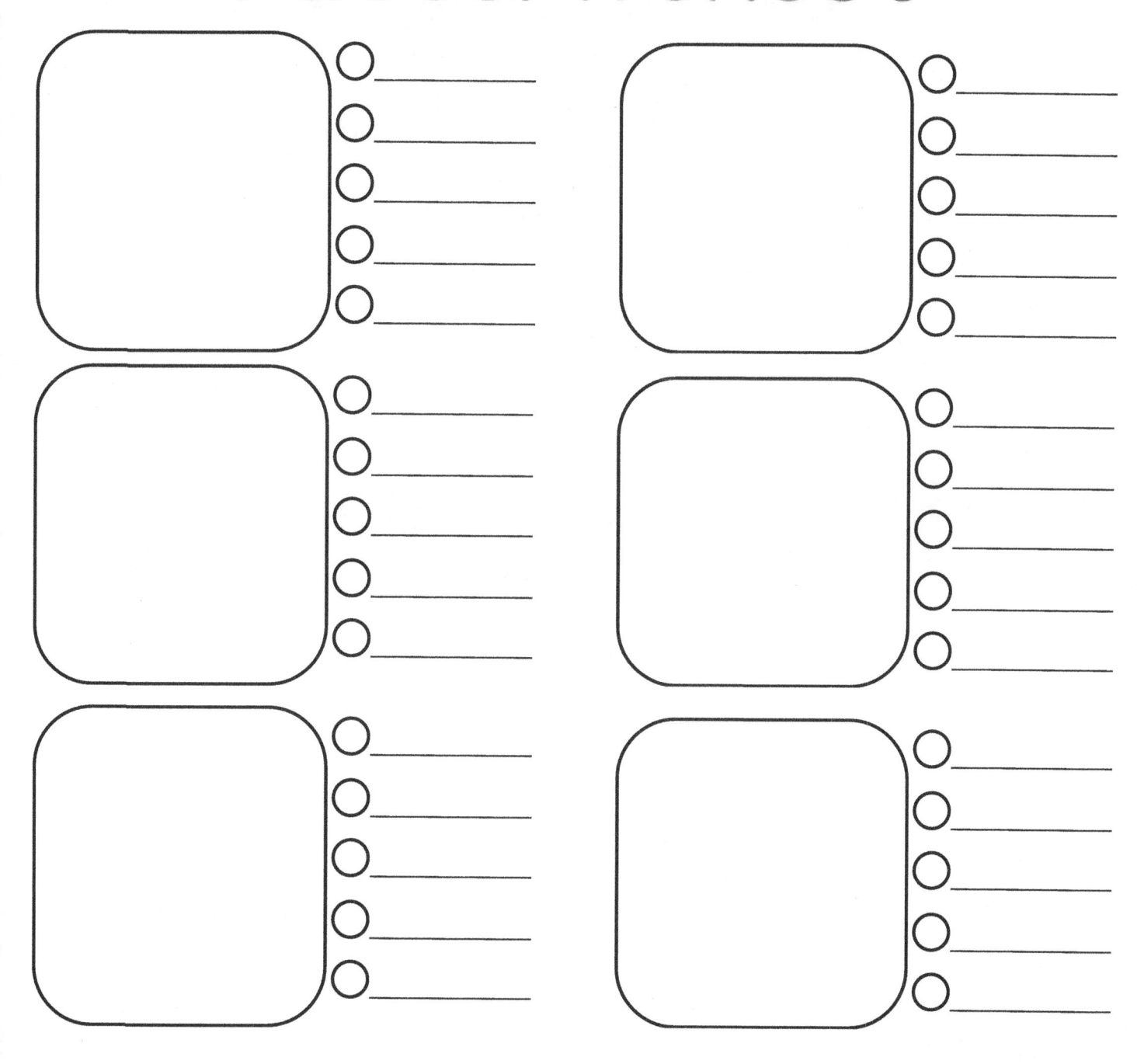

Pattern Sheet

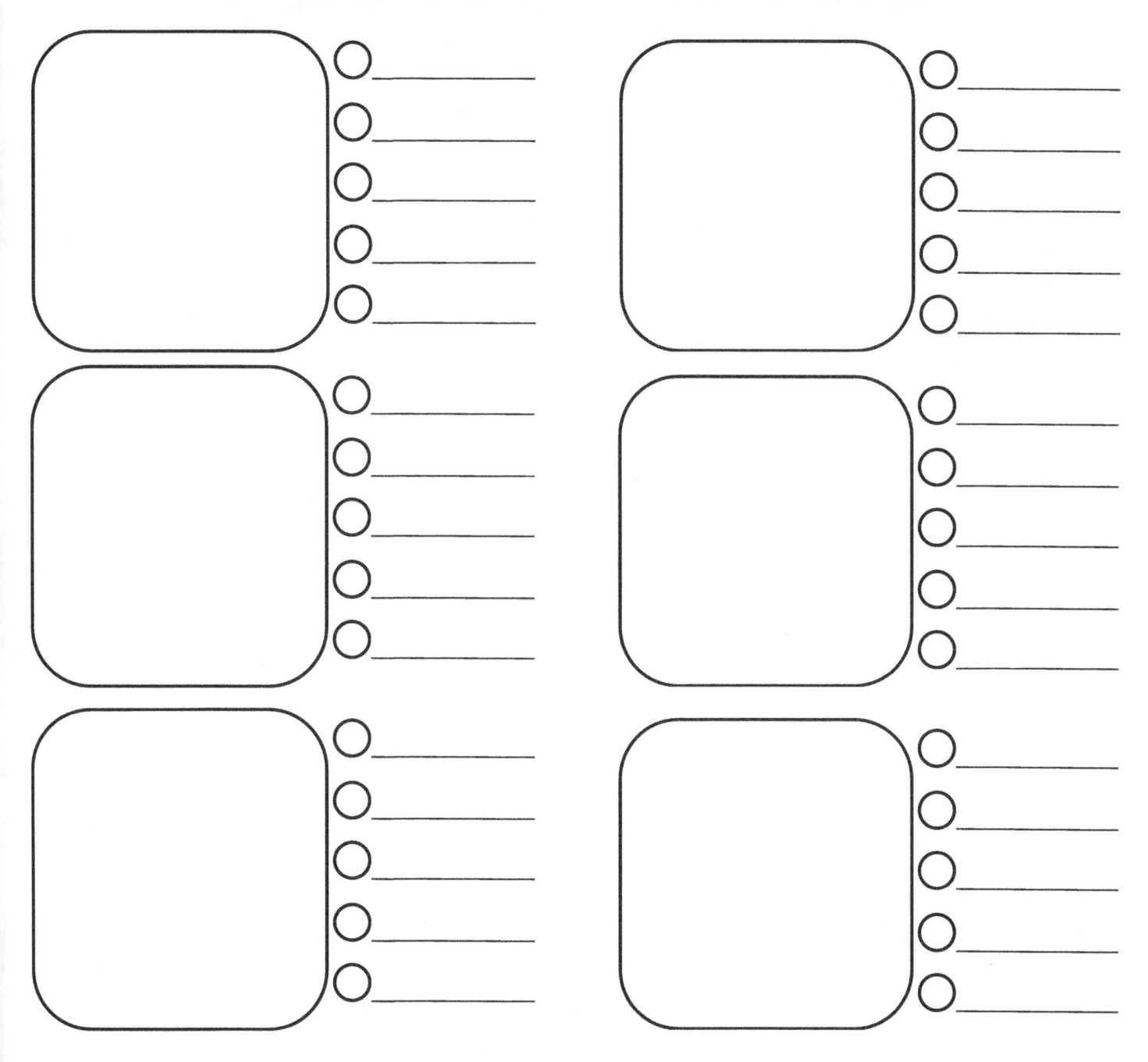

Pattern Sheet

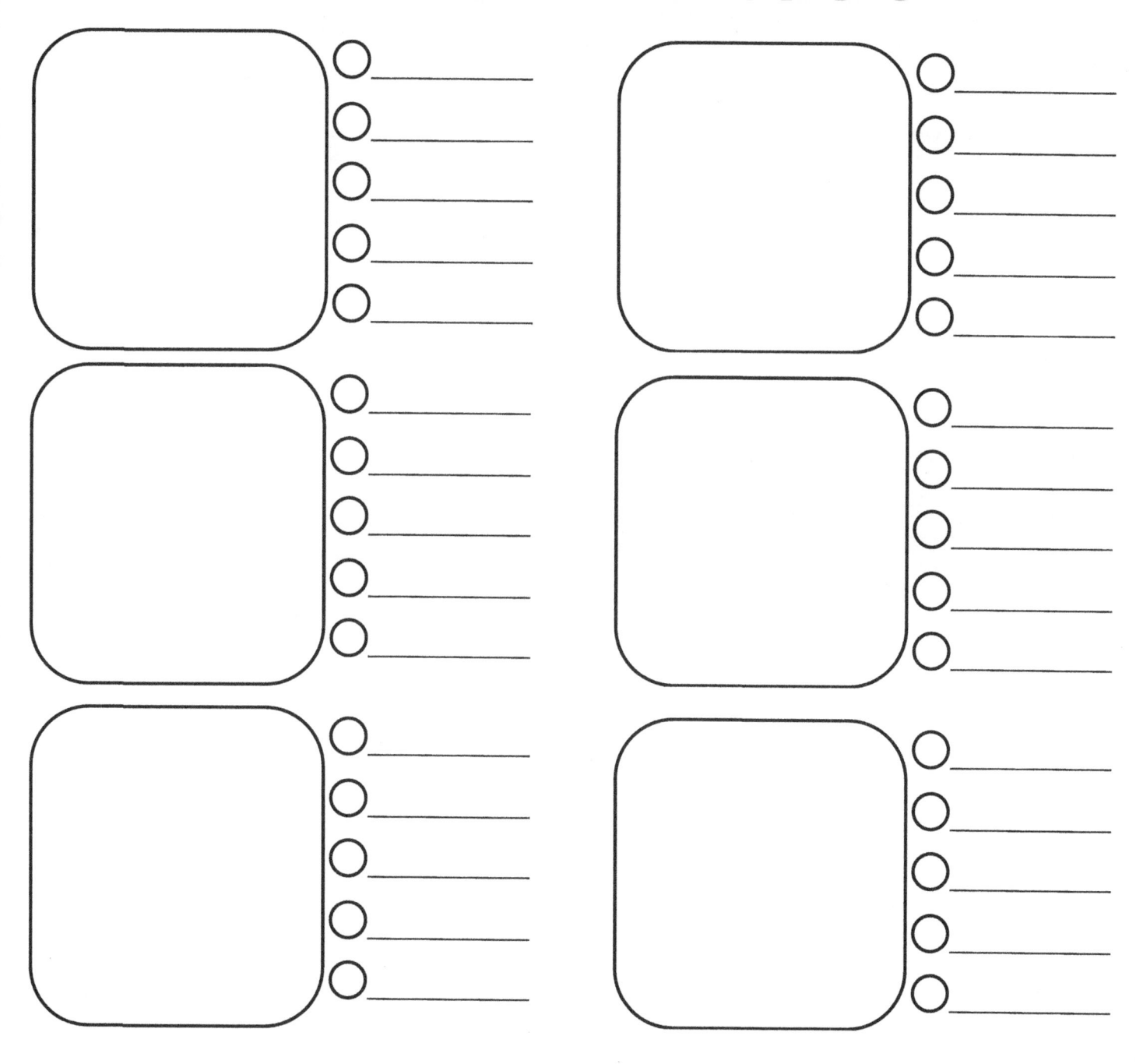

Pattern Sheet

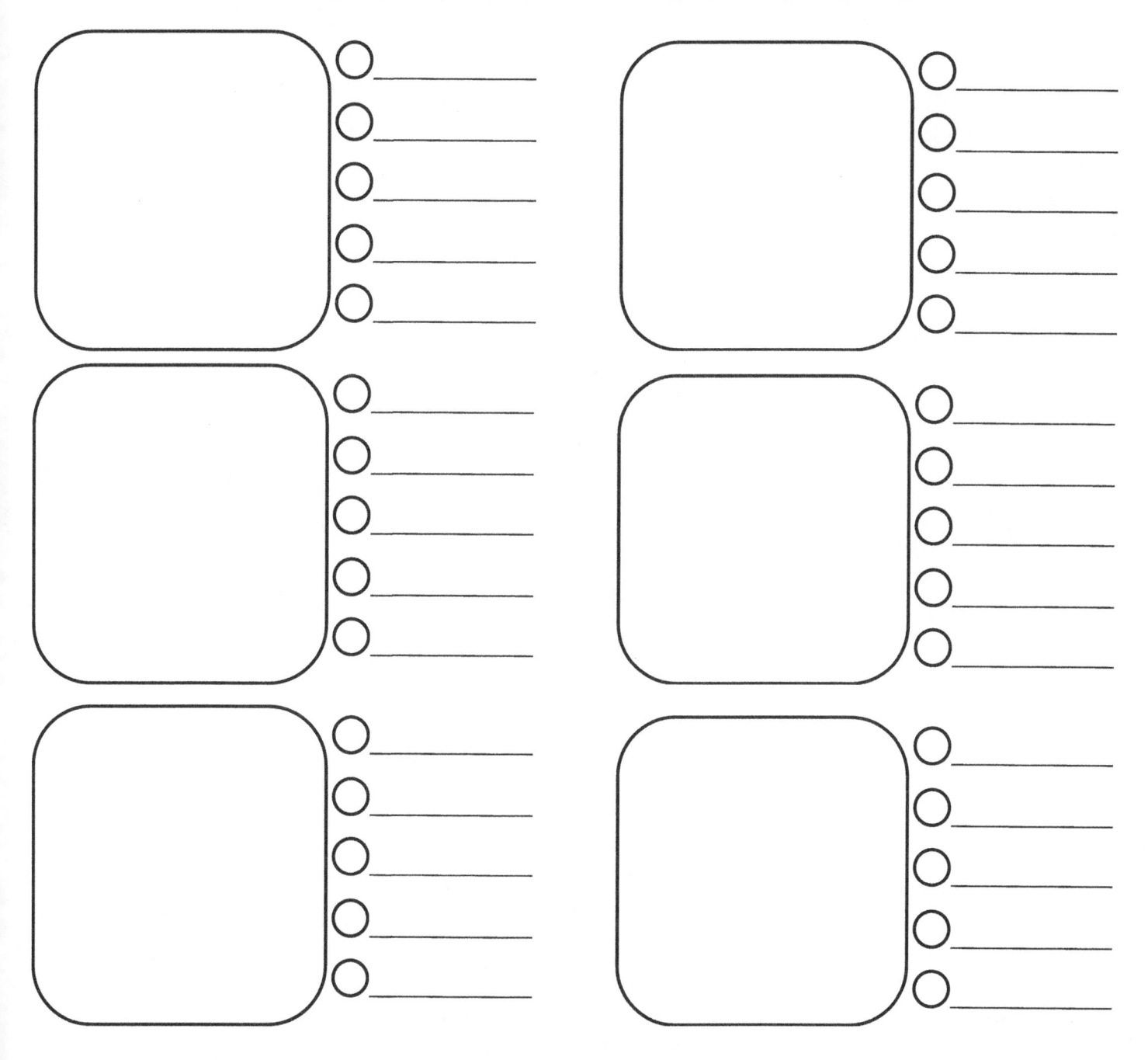

Blending

Blending

Blending

Blending

Night Sky

Create deep night scenes with stars, constellations, or galaxies

color swatches

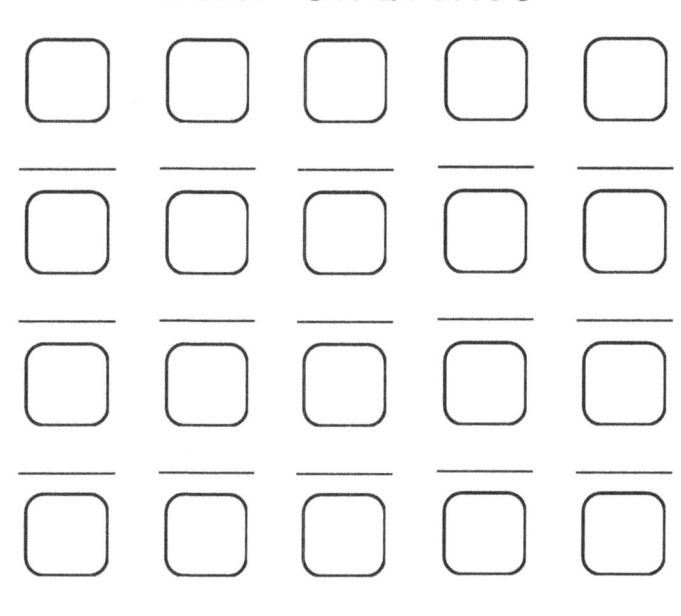

Try blending dark blues and purples to create starry night sky

Night sky

Create deep night scenes with stars, constellations, or galaxies

color swatches

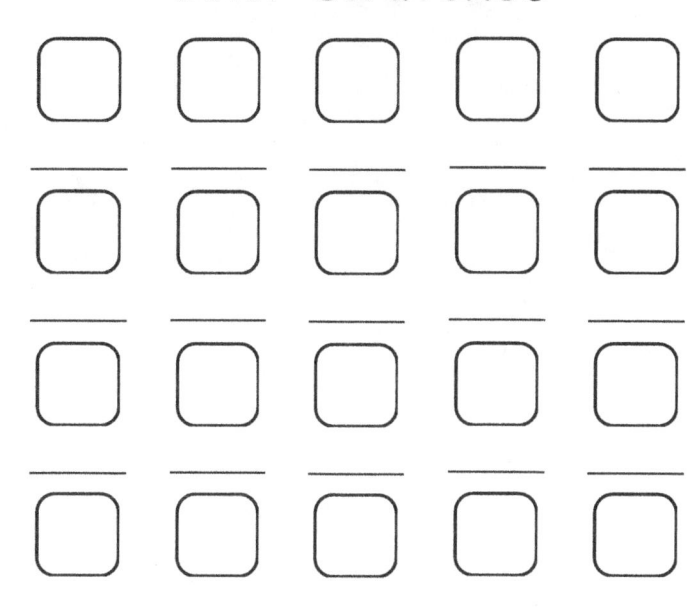

Try blending dark blues and purples to create starry night sky

Night Sky

Create deep night scenes with stars, constellations, or galaxies

color swatches

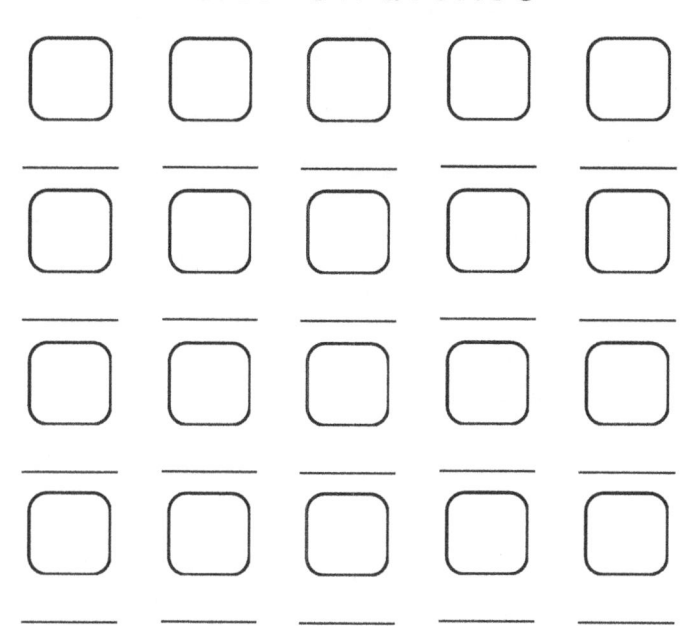

Try blending dark blues and purples to create starry night sky

shadow cast

Practice shadow direction from a specific light source

color swatches

Add shadow or light effect to match the direction of light source

shadow cast

Practice shadow direction from a specific light source

color swatches

Add shadow or light effect to match the direction of light source

shadow cast

Practice shadow direction from a specific light source

color swatches

Add shadow or light effect to match the direction of light source

Fabric surface

Shades crease & folds to create soft, flowing textiles

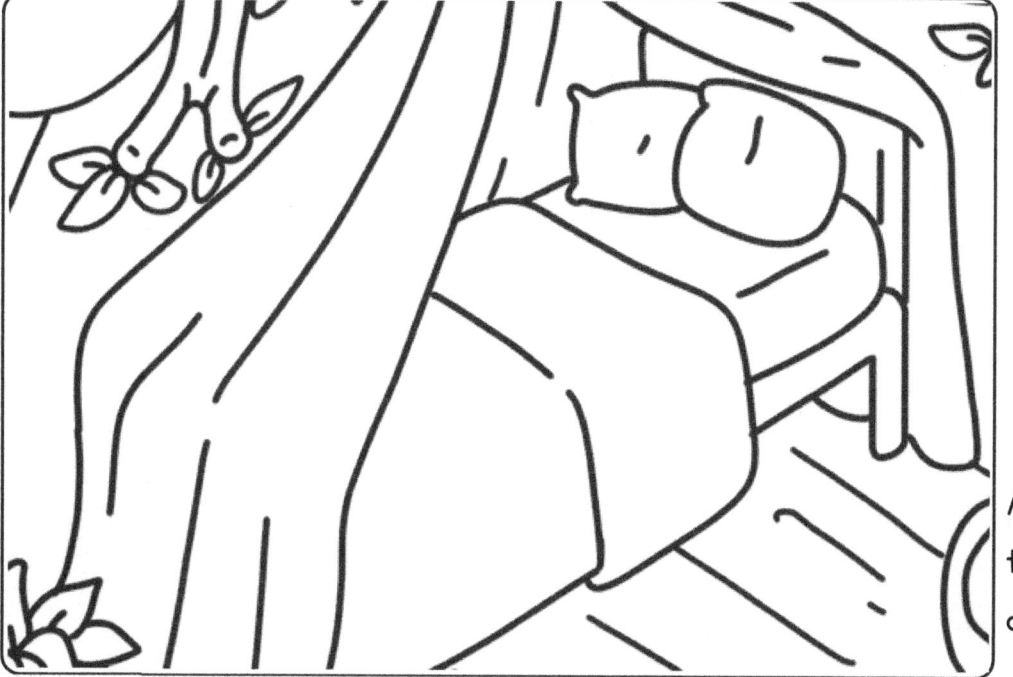

color swatches

Add patterns & shadows to the fabric for realistic apperance

Fabric surface

Shades crease & folds to create soft, flowing textiles

color swatches

Add patterns & shadows to the fabric for realistic apperance

Fabric surface

Shades crease & folds to create soft, flowing textiles

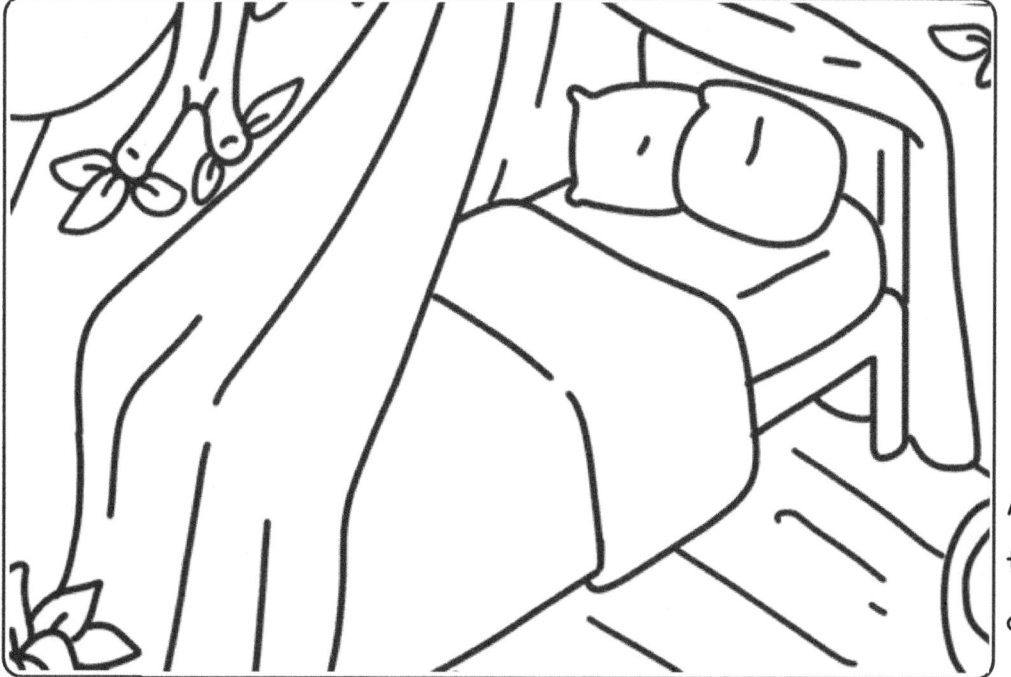

color swatches

Add patterns & shadows to the fabric for realistic apperance

water & Bubbles

Design water surfaces, water foams & bubble for realistic appearance

color swatches

Test & design water surface, foams & bubbles to make realistic water movement

Water & Bubbles

Design water surfaces, water foams & bubble for realistic appearance

color swatches

Test & design water surface, foams & bubbles to make realistic water movement

water & Bubbles

Design water surfaces, water foams & bubble for realistic appearance

color swatches

Test & design water surface, foams & bubbles to make realistic water movement

Snow & Frost

Draw snow piles or snowflakes and create frosty effects to make it look cold outside

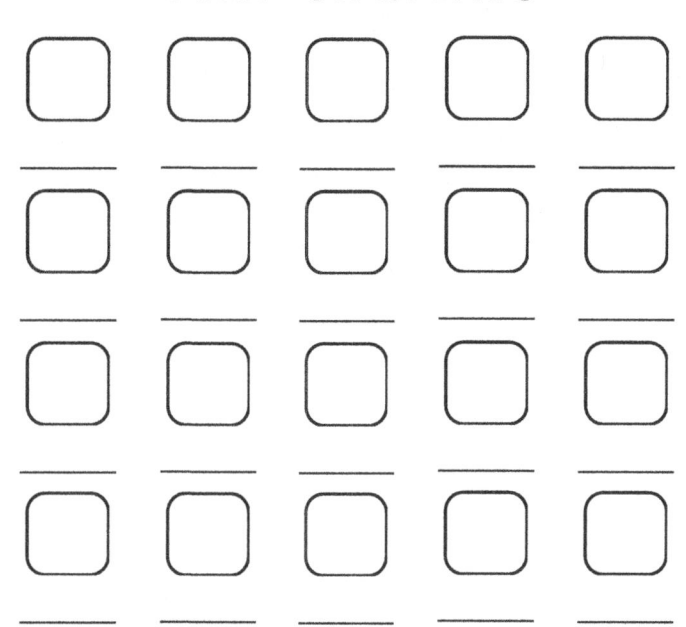

color swatches

Add snow and make window frost effect

Snow & Frost

Draw snow piles or snowflakes and create frosty effects to make it look cold outside

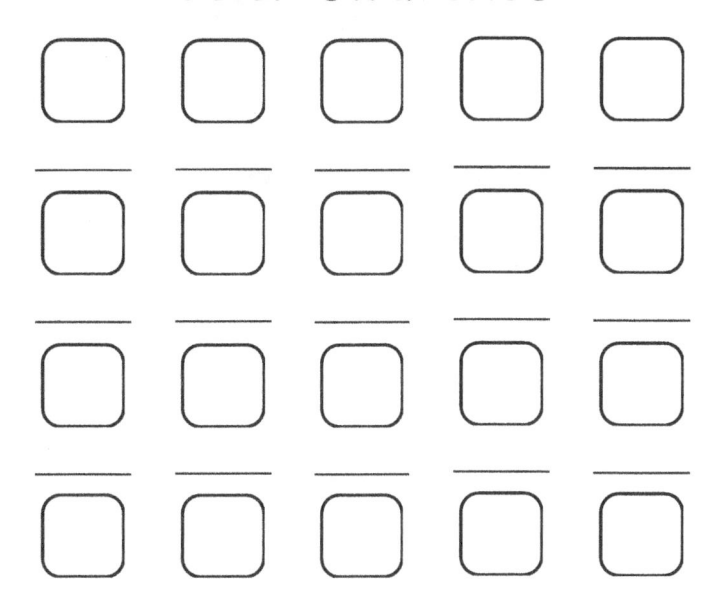

color swatches

Add snow and make window frost effect

Snow & Frost

Draw snow piles or snowflakes and create frosty effects to make it look cold outside

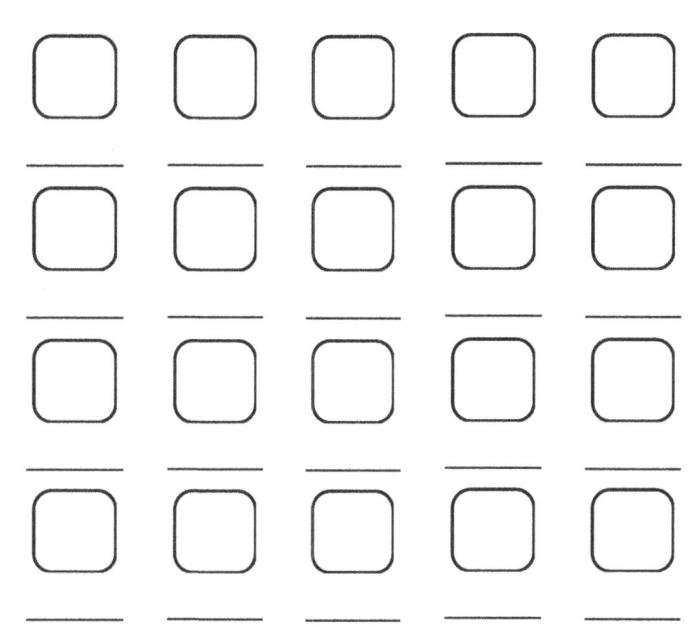

color swatches

Add snow and make window frost effect

stone path

Shade color gradient, make the stone pattern to create stone path appearance

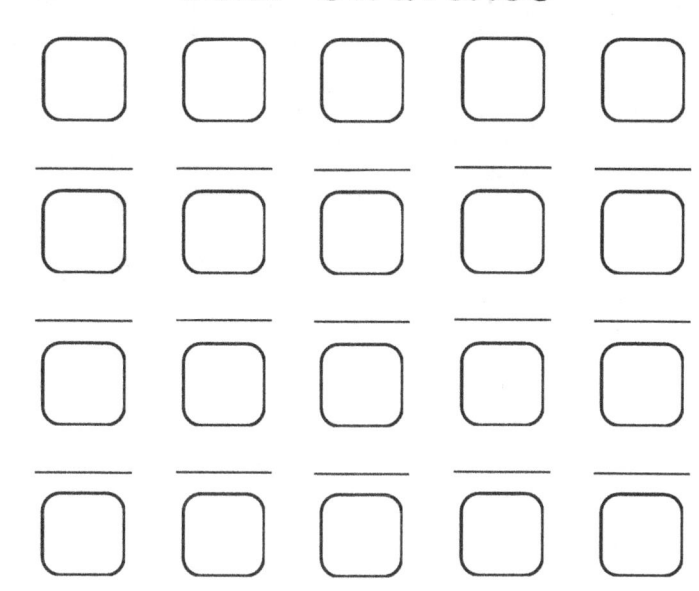

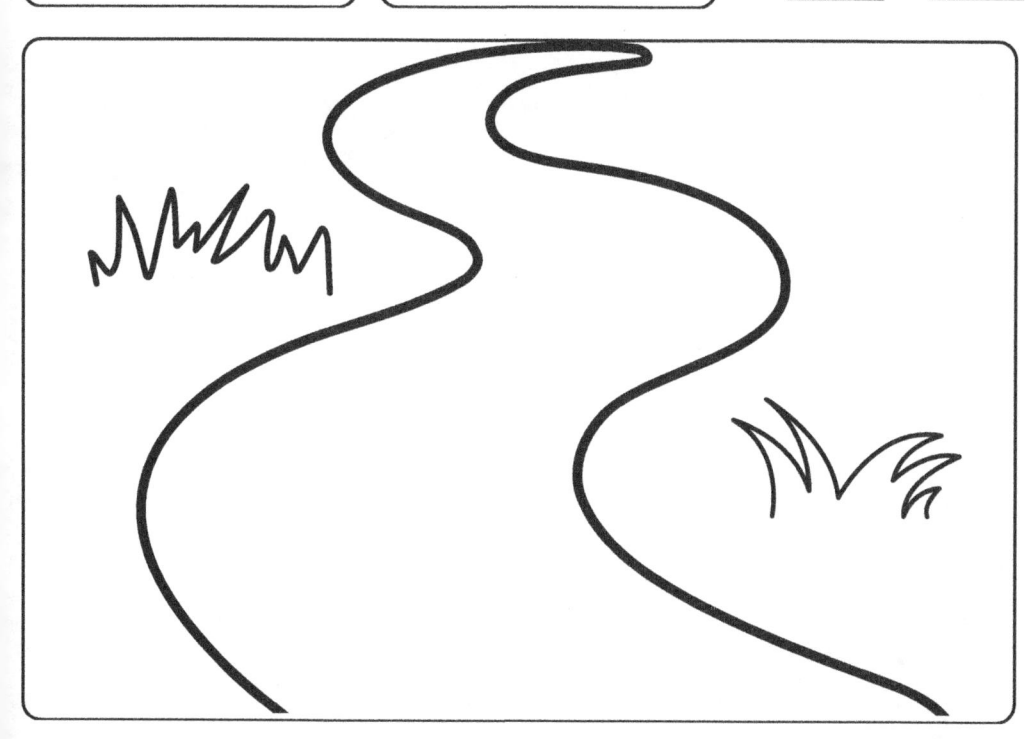

color swatches

create stone pattern on the given path

stone path

Shade color gradient, make the stone pattern to create stone path appearance

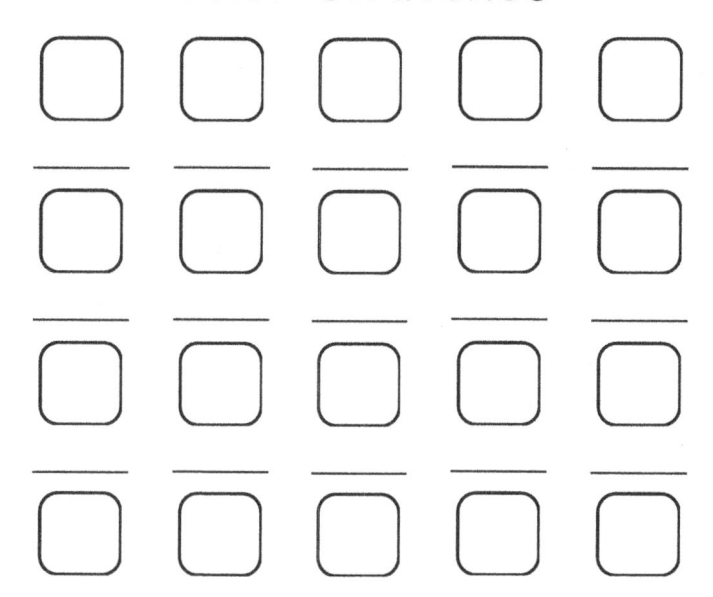

color swatches

create stone pattern on the given path

stone path

Shade color gradient, make the stone pattern to create stone path appearance

color swatches

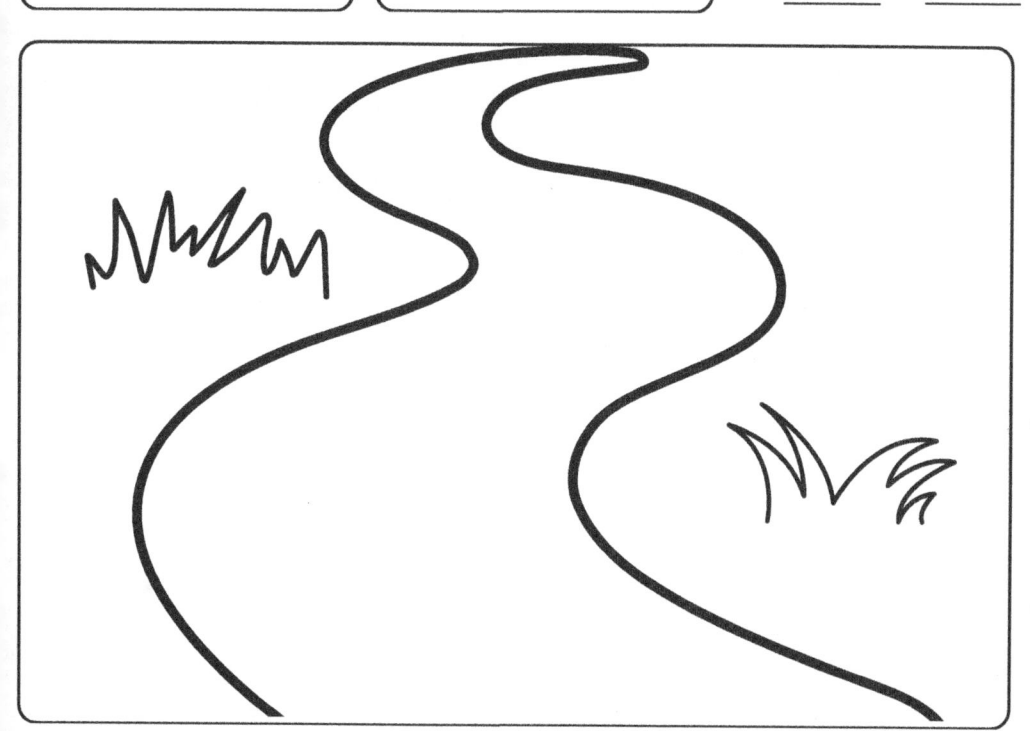

create stone pattern on the given path

Invisible object

Imagine the background drawing to make an invisible object

color swatches

create outline to make this ghost look transparent

Invisible Object

Imagine the background drawing to make an invisible object

color swatches

create outline to make this ghost look transparent

Invisible object

Imagine the background drawing to make an invisible object

color swatches

create outline to make this ghost look transparent

tree

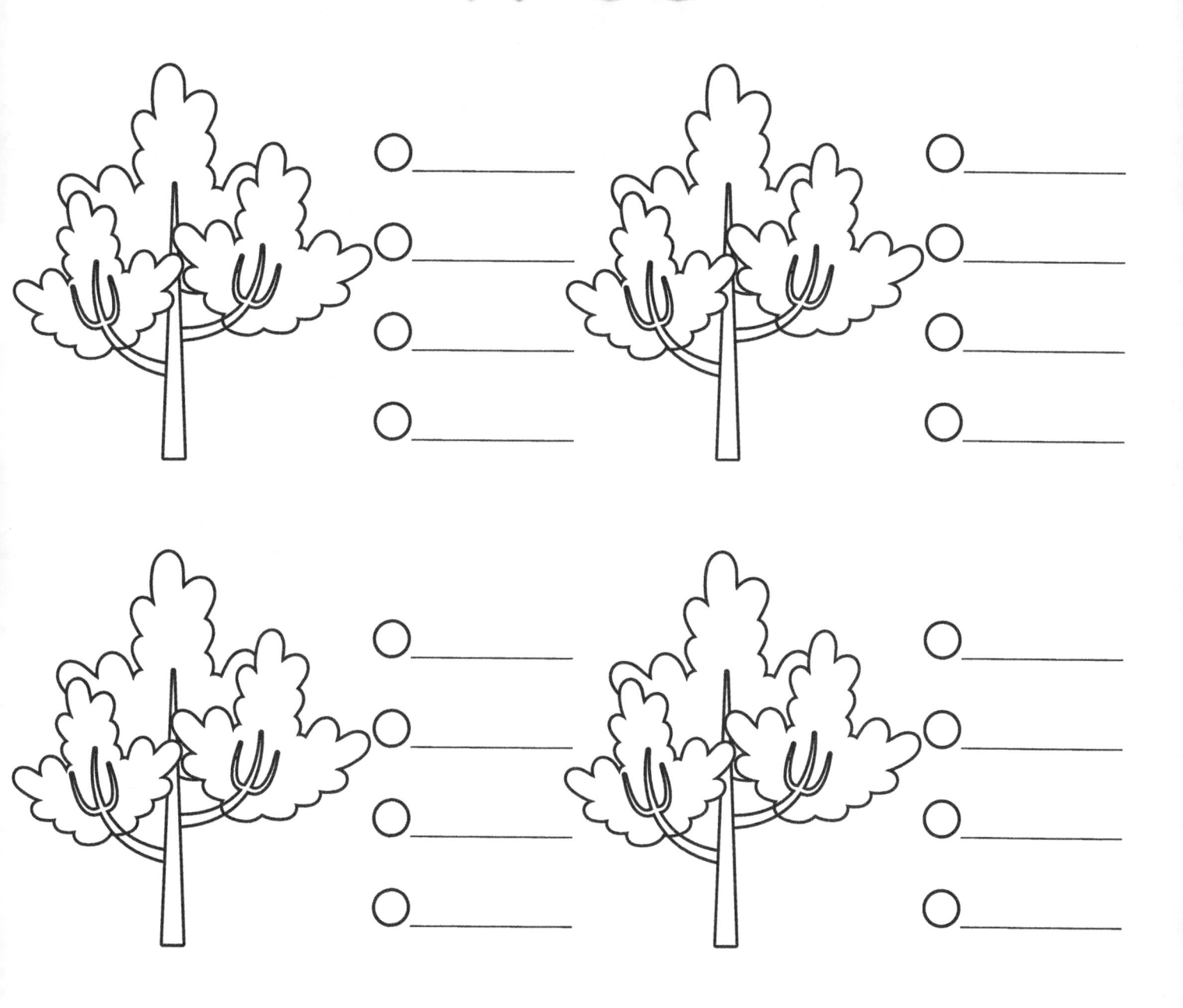

Tree

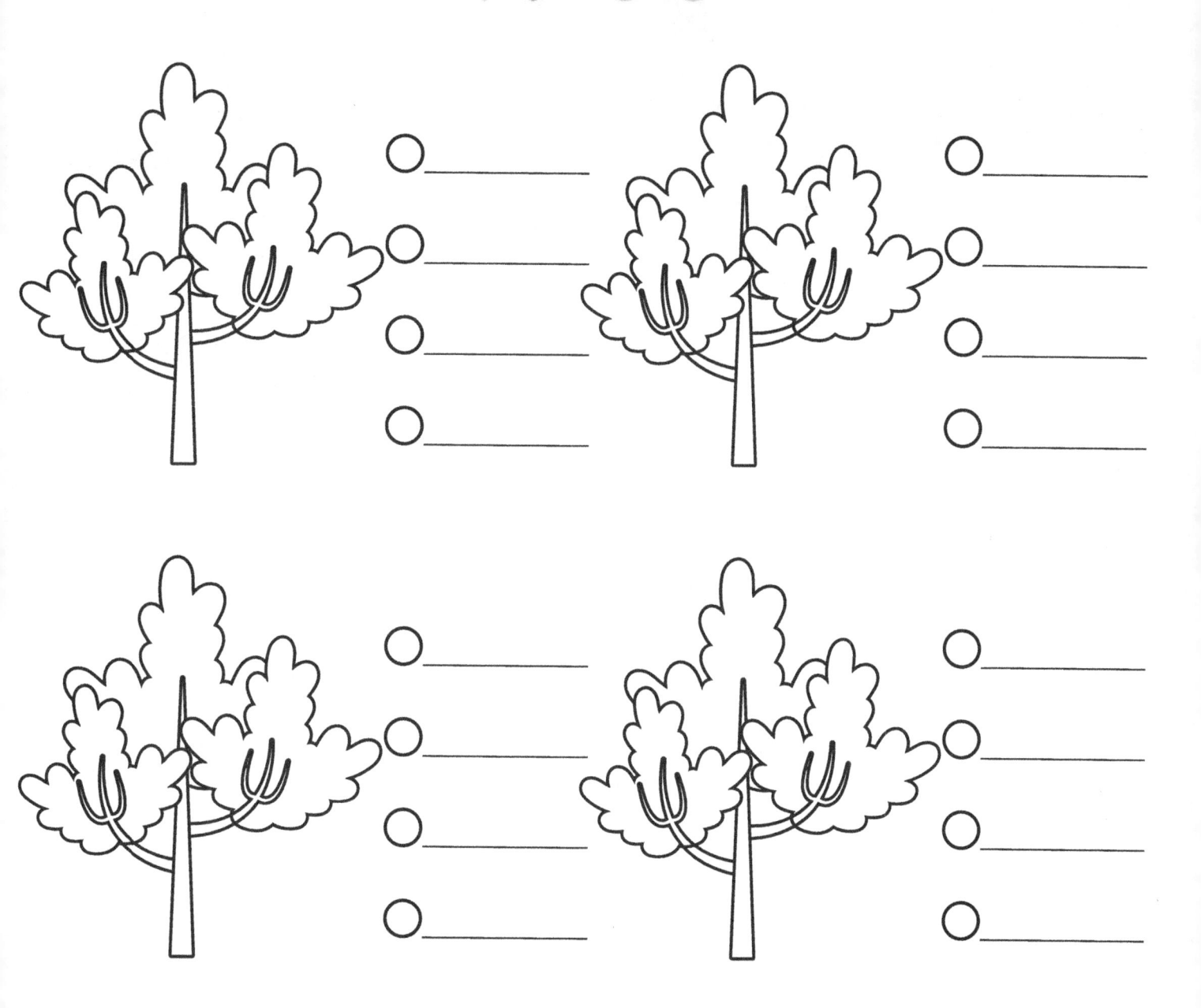

○ _____
○ _____
○ _____
○ _____

○ _____
○ _____
○ _____
○ _____

○ _____
○ _____
○ _____
○ _____

○ _____
○ _____
○ _____
○ _____

tree

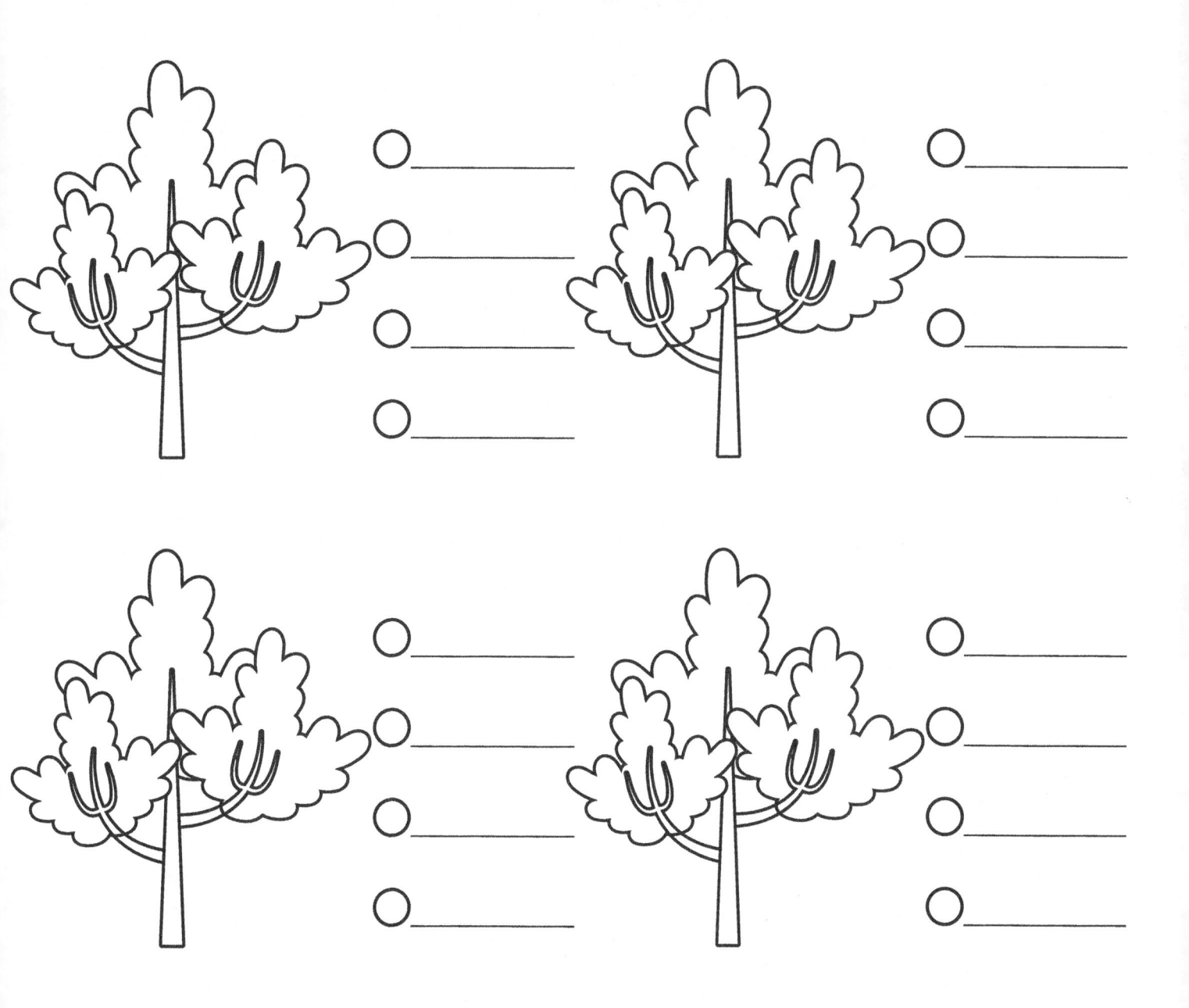

Hair

Hair

Hair

window

Window

Window

dog

dog

dog

Brick

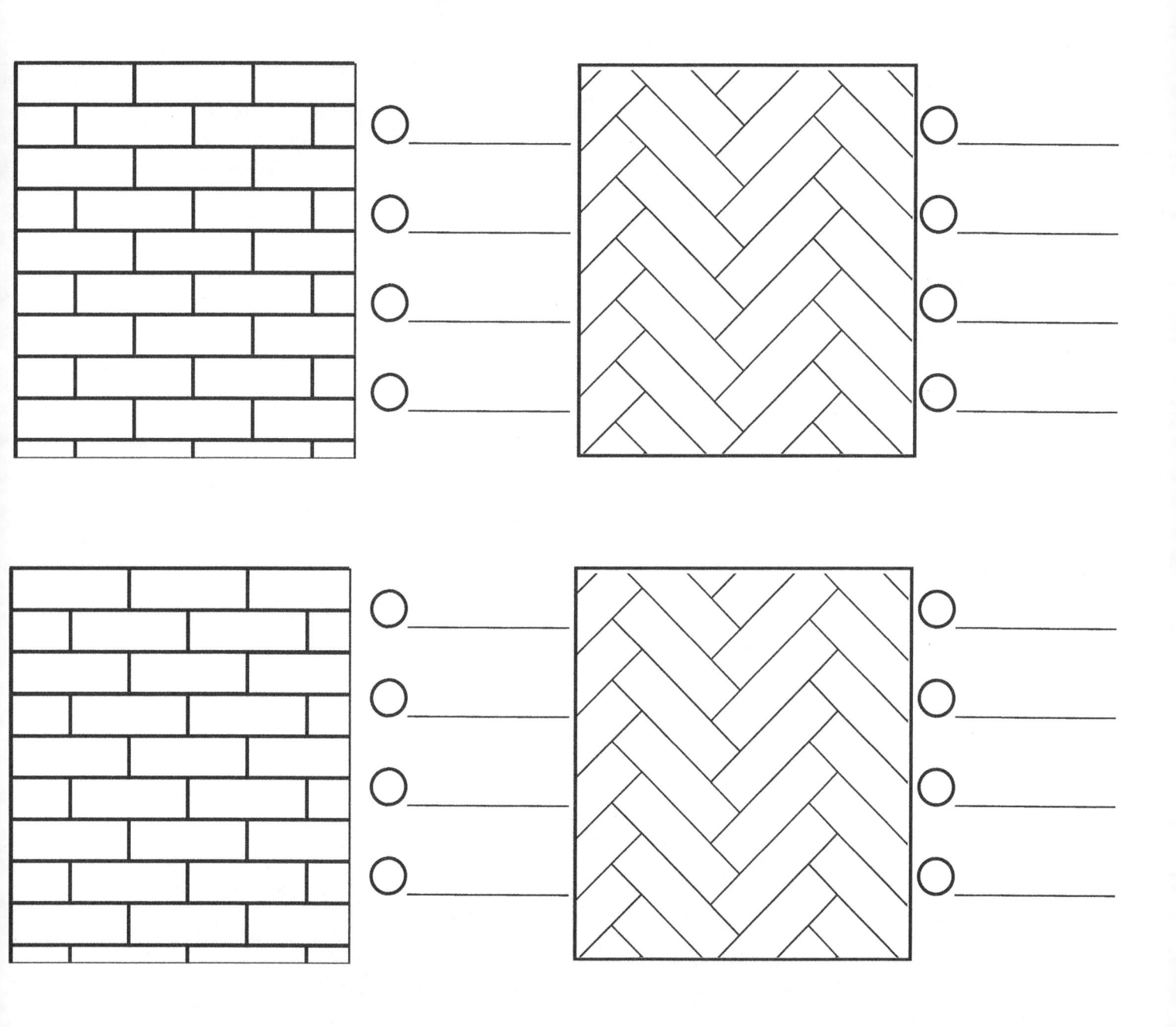

Brick

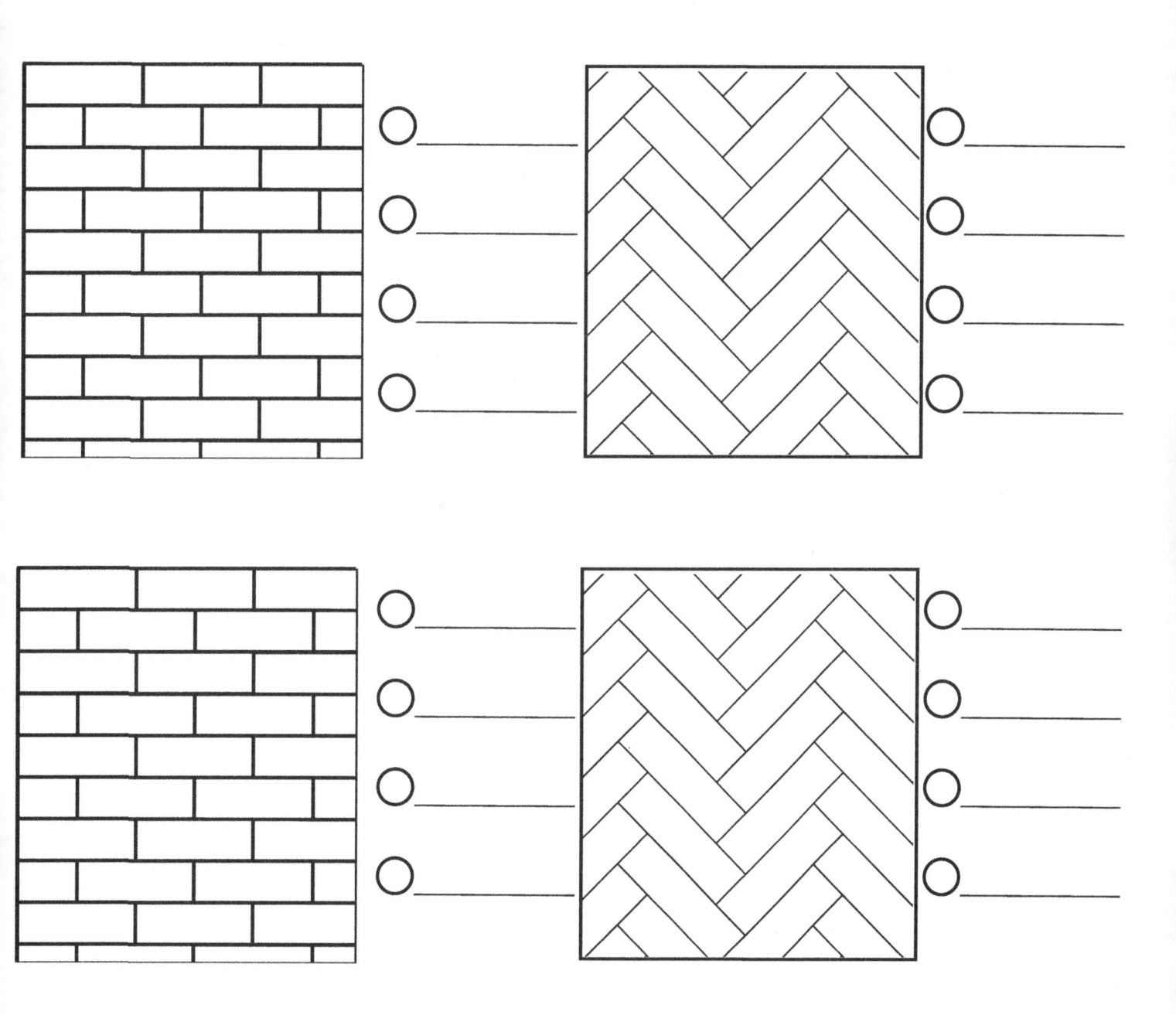

Brick

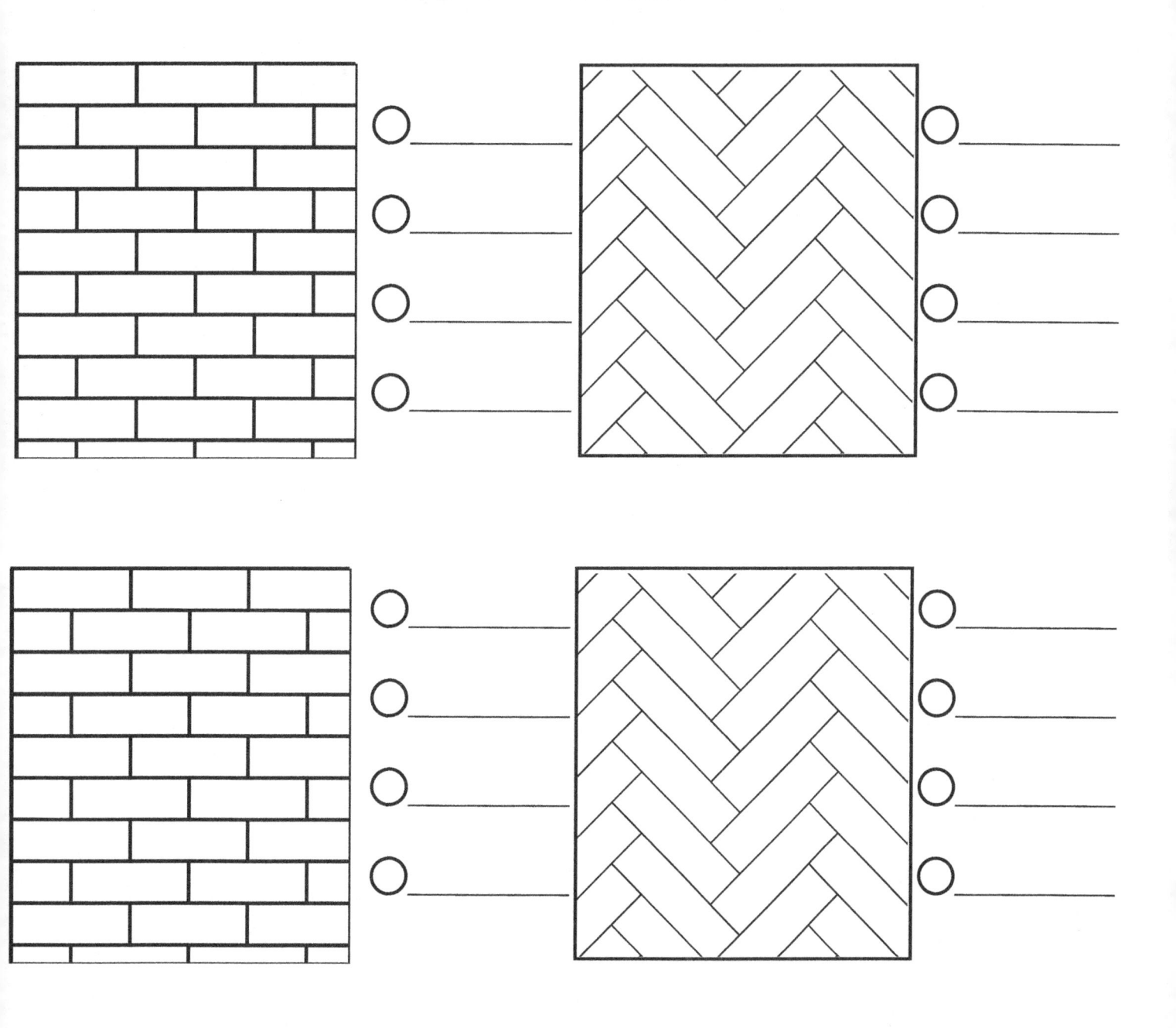

Made in the USA
Las Vegas, NV
08 March 2025